S0-AXX-648

Giovanna Magi

MASADA
and the Dead Sea

JERICHO - KHIRBET QUMRAN - EIN GEDI

BONECHI & STEIMATZKY

© Copyright 1993 by Casa Editrice Bonechi, via Cairoli 18/b Florence - Italy - Tel. 55/576841 - Telex 571323 CEB - Fax (55)5000766
All rights reserved. No part of this book my be reproduced without the written permission of the Publisher.
Printed in Italy by Centro Stampa Editoriale Bonechi.
Translated by Erika Pauli, Studio Comunicare, Florence.

Photographs from the Archives of Casa Editrice Bonechi taken by Paolo Giambone.
Color plates on pages 29 above and 45 are due to Stefano Benini.

ISBN 88-7009-960-1

The oasis of Jericho glowing green in the Judean desert.

JERICHO

« And the people came up out of Jordan on the tenth day of the first month and encamped in Gilgal, in the east border of Jericho » (Joshua 4:19) and *« ...and when the people heard the sound of the trumpet... the wall fell down flat... and they took the city. And they utterly destroyed all that was in the city, both man and woman, young and old, and ox, and sheep, and ass, with the edge of the sword. »* (Joshua 6:20-21).

This is one of the best known passages in the Bible, describing how Jericho, *« the city of the palms »* (Judges, 3:13) was besieged by the Israelites under the leadership of Joshua, and how for seven days the ark was carried in procession and all the trumpets of his army were blown until on the seventh day the mighty walls fell.

This exploit of the Hebrews on their way towards the Promised Land made the city famous, but in terms of archaeology Jericho holds a record, for it is considered the most ancient city in the world.

Jericho, a dazzling green oasis surrounded on all sides by the deserted arid plain, ten kilometers north of the Dead Sea, was already visited by man all of 12,000 years ago, when it was a seasonal stopover for groups of nomad hunters. In the 10th millennium the presence of man became stable. The knowledge of Jericho's ancient history is the result of a series of archaeological digs on the mound of Tell es-Sultan. The first real campaign was that of Ernst Sellin and Carl Watzinger in 1907, followed — in 1929 — by that of John Garstang and finally, in the early 1950s, by that of the

The Judean desert and the monastery of St. George at Kotziba.

The oasis of Jericho dominated by Gebel Qarantal, or the Mount of the Temptations.

great Kathleen Kenyon, head of the British School of Archaeology in Jerusalem.

All these archaeological campaigns established that the earliest construction dated to about 9250 B.C. and consisted of an oval building, almost a natural evolution from the pre-existing rush hut.

By 7000 B.C. the community of hunters had turned to agriculture and the semi-nomad settlement became sedentary. The urban nucleus of Jericho stretched out over about four hectares, with a wall three meters thick and at least four meters high. The mighty defense tower measured nine meters across and the top (about eight and a half meters) was reached by an internal staircase. This period is called pre-ceramic Neolithic I: man practised agriculture but did not yet use clay utensils. Development continued in the second phase of pre-ceramic Neolithic with houses that were now rectangular in plan and with rooms that were grouped around spacious courtyards where traces of hearths indicate that food was cooked. The walls were in sun-baked brick, plastered and colored in various shades of red and orange and the floors were in beaten earth with interesting finishing touches which allowed water to flow off. The larger rooms were flanked by other smaller ones without openings, which were probably used for storing provisions.

The most important find was a human skull (seven others subsequently also came to light) covered by a thick layer of plaster and with pieces of shell in the orbital cavities: unquestionably an interesting form of ancestor worship.

Around 5000 B.C. new inhabitants settled in Jericho, introducing pottery, terracotta ware glazed in red and with incised designs. When this phase, called ceramic Neolithic, came to an end, apparently sometime in the second half of the 5th millennium, Jericho was aban-

Three views of the archaeological zone of Jericho, the oldest city in the world.

doned for reasons still unknown until about 3200 B.C. At the beginning of the Early Bronze Age man returned to the site and remained throughout the Middle Bronze Age: the encircling walls, almost seventeen meters high and surrounding an area of almost two hectares, were destroyed and reconstructed, in the course of a thousand years, at least seventeen times. The city was subject not only to the attacks of enemies, but also to frequent violent earthquakes. The well-known Bible episode of the fall of the famous walls was the result of an earthquake. At least this is what the archaeologist Garstang concluded after noting that the external bastion had collapsed outside along the slope, while the internal bastion had collapsed in the opposite direction. The walls also had large fissures. Repeatedly abandoned and reconstructed, destroyed by the Babylonians — who deported the inhabitants in 587 —, in Roman times the oasis of Jericho was famous for its wealth: the spring of sweet water, the date palms and above all the resin of the trees. The balsam of Galaad was rich in medicinal properties, a cure for headaches and cataracts, and one of the major exports of Judea. Marc Antony gave the oasis to Cleopatra, but Herod succeeded in getting it back and exploiting the cultivations for his personal use. It was under this king, who died there in 4 B.C., that Jericho experienced a period of great splendor. Herod had a hippodrome, an amphitheatre and above all a winter residence of rare beauty built there. A mild climate, luxuriant vegetation and an abundance of water, had made this oasis a real paradise, where the Hashmonean sovereigns of the 2nd century B.C., who spent their winters here, had perfected an extraordinary irrigation system.

On these pages, four pictures of the excavations of Tell es-Sultan which brought to light an imposing bastion with foundations that date to 7000 B.C.

The spring of Ain es-Sultan.

The mosaics that have come to light in the buildings in Jericho testify to the great skill of the mosaicists. Above, right: the mosaic of the ancient Synagogue. At the center is the Menorah, symbol of Israel, and the words « Shalom al Israel », which mean Peace be on Israel.

SPRING OF AIN ES-SULTAN
(Sultan's well)

About two miles north-west of modern Jericho, has from times immemorable watered the flourishing vegetation of the oasis and is traditionally identified with the well of Elijah. In II Kings (2:19-22) it is told how: « ...the men of the city said unto Elisha, Behold, I pray thee, the situation of this city is pleasant, as my lord seeth: but the water is naught, and the ground barren. And he said, Bring me a new cruse, and put salt therein. And they brought it to him. And he went forth unto the spring of the waters, and cast the salt in there, and said, Thus saith the Lord, I have healed these waters; there shall not be from thence any more death or barren land. So the waters were healed unto this day, according to the saying of Elisha which he spake. ».

But Jericho is also bound to the name of Jesus, who passed there near the end of his ministry.

The mound of Old Jericho (Tell es-Sultan) is dominated by the imposing rocky mass of Gebel Qarantal, identified with the Mount of the Temptation. Jericho is also the place where « Zacchaeus... the chief among the publicans, and... rich » met Jesus and repented (Luke, 19:2) and near which the blind beggar Bartimaeus had his sight restored (Mark, 10:46-52).

A few details of the sumptuous palace of Hisham.

THE PALACE OF HISHAM

Two kilometers north of Jericho, in Kirbet Mafjar, is the capricious « castle in the desert » of the Omayyad caliph Hisham Ib'n Abed el Malik, whose principal residence was in Damascus. The palace was built between 724 and 743 A.D. — twenty years to create this extraordinary complex of apartments, baths, pools, colonnades, courtyards, etc. The bath house contains the famous mosaic known as the « *tree of life* », perhaps the loveliest to be found in the region, where the enchantment of nature and a primitive Eden mingle with an acute observation of reality.

It is said that on account of the extravagance of forms and the not particularly orthodox decoration, the designer of this palace was the nephew of the sultan, Walid ibn Yazid, whose dissolute life in the company of actors and whose propensity for drinking bouts had led to his being exiled from court. Unfortunately, in 747 A.D., barely four years after it was finished, a violent earthquake razed the caliph's summer residence to the ground: many objects have been taken to the Rockefeller Museum in Jerusalem. Still to be seen here however is the extraordinary airiness of the architecture, the elegance of the decorative details, the wealth of ornamentation, the luxury of the premises.

The remains of a great hall in the palace of Hisham, with slender engaged columns on the pillars.

Detail of a building with a fine mosaic pavement and a niche flanked by two small columns.

A view of the baths with a detail of the rich decoration.

Two pictures of the pool.

The entrance to the excavations and a view over the caves from on high.

KHIRBET QUMRAN

It is the irony of fate that what has been defined as « the greatest find of manuscripts in modern times » came about by pure chance and was made not by an archaeologist, but by a young shepherd of the Bedouin tribe of the Taamira. One spring day in 1947 Mohammed adh-Dhib (« Mohammed the Wolf ») was out looking for a goat which had strayed in that desolate and impervious region which lies between Jerusalem and the western banks of the Dead Sea. Thinking the animal was hiding in one of the many grottoes in the rocks, the boy threw a stone into one of the openings and heard the sound of breaking shards. Frightened, he ran away, to return the next day with a friend. They entered the cave and found many terracotta amphoras which contained parchment scrolls in linen wrappings. Hoping they were worth something, the scrolls were taken to the market in Bethlehem, where they passed through various hands, but none of the merchants at the time recognized their enormous value.

The scrolls were divided into two lots: the first, which contained five, was taken to Metropolite Anasthasius Yeshue Samuel, the Syrian Orthodox Archbishop of the monastery of Saint Mark in Jerusalem; the second lot — three scrolls — was bought by Prof. Sukenik of the Hebrew University of Jerusalem, after long and extenuating negotiations. Once he had carefully examined the parchment scrolls, Sukenik realized not only that they were authentic, but above all that they were manuscripts dating to the period of the Second Temple, prior, therefore, by at least a thousand years to the oldest Hebrew manuscripts known up to then.

The three scrolls in his possession, written in ancient Hebrew and Aramaic Greek, turned out to be the *Books of Isaiah*, the *Scroll of Thanksgiving Psalms* and the *Scroll of the War of the Sons of Light with the Sons of Darkness*. Four other scrolls contained *Commentaries on Habakkuk*, the *Manual of Discipline*, the *Genesis Apocryphon* and the second *Book of Isaiah*: all the books of the Old Testament except Esther.

It was a truly extraordinary discovery, for up to then the soil of that land had yielded materials such as met-

Two views of the ruins of Qumran.

al, terracotta, ivory but never before parchment.

But who had written these scrolls, and why? The answer came only two years later when two archaeologists, Father Roland de Vaux and G. Harding, succeeded in entering the area and rigorously carrying out scientific excavations.

Here, in a landscape of apocalyptic beauty, burned by the sun and devoid of vegetation, caught between the steep slopes of the Judean Desert on the west and the immobility of the Dead Sea on the east, the remains of a monastic settlement which had reached its zenith between 150 B.C. and 68 A.D. came to light. The community which had inhabited this inhospitable site was that of the Essenes, a Hebrew sect which had sought refuge here from the worldliness of Jerusalem, far from the intrigues and pomp of the court dominated by the Hashmonean dynasty. They interpreted literally the prophesy of Isaiah (40:3) « *Prepare ye the way of the Lord, make straight in the desert a highway for our God* », and here, following doctrinal and ritual models unbelievably similar to those of the early Christians, they preached a life of purity and ascetism. The Essene beliefs can perhaps be considered the purest expression of Hebrew monotheism: the followers of the « Teacher of Righteousness », as the founder of the sect was called, communally divided the fruits of their labors, practised purificatory rites such as baptism and ritual ablutions, meditated on the Holy Scriptures in expectation of the ultimate end of the world. Their ideals are described by Flavius Josephus, in chapter VIII of book I of « *The Jewish Wars* »: *They reject pleasure as an evil, while temperance and resistance to passions are virtues... they avoid the pleasures of the senses... They spurn wealth and hold all their goods in common... they are particularly pious with regards to God... ».*

Pliny the Elder also mentions them in his *Naturalis Historia*, localizing them with great precision: « *The Essenes live to the west of the Dead Sea... below them lay the city of Engaddi... from whence the fortress of Masada on the rock is reached... ».*

In the course of five archaeological campaigns, the monastic complex of Khirbet Qumran was brought to light.

The community ate their meals, which were ritual in character, together in public; the room reserved for the communal meal was also purified with water, of particular note when one considers the extreme aridity of the zone in which the Essenes had chosen to live. But the ancient inhabitants of Qumran were well organized: an ingenious system of conduits and cisterns collected and conserved the water that overflowed from the steep « wadi » during the rainy season. Once purified in a large decantation basin, it was channeled to seven large cisterns which distributed it to all the rooms in the monastery.

Excavations have made it possible to identify the various rooms that served the needs of the community. They included a kitchen, storerooms, a refectory, and above all the vast scriptorium in which the famous Scrolls found later in the caves in the surroundings had been written. The room had narrow brick and stucco tables on which the scribes stretched the animal skins that had been previously cleaned and tanned. The ink was a mixture of charcoal and gum and was kept in clay or bronze inkwells. The desks also had recipients for water, used by the scribe to purify his fingers every time he came across the word YHWH (God) in the text he was copying.

Once finished, the scrolls were sealed, individually wrapped in linen wrappings and put inside clay amphoras: a sign that whoever hid them did all in his power to preserve them. But in other caves the material was not laid away with the same care and it therefore appears that an unexpected event had forced the Essenes to abandon the zone in great haste. Probably the direct cause was the Judean War, when the Roman legions laid waste to the region. Almost certainly many of the Essenes who survived fled for a last stand to Masada, where they died heroically defending the fort. The great quantity of manuscripts found in the caves

around Khirbet Qumran — cave n. 4 alone has furnished about six hundred fragments of the books of Isaiah, Samuel I and Samuel II — has aided the archaeologists in their excavations, for in their authenticity these manuscripts documented the remains that were being unearthed. Even more, however, they cast new light on the history of Christianity and Judaism.

Some objects from the Cave of the Letters and a detail of the Temple Scroll.

The rocky landscape on all sides of the excavations of Khirbet Qumran.

The Dead Sea seen from the ruins of Masada and two pictures of the rock.

MASADA

Masada: a name which is much more than an extraordinary archaeological adventure. Masada is a symbol, one of those collective memories which have permitted the Hebrew peoples to maintain a national identity above and beyond the thousand frontiers beyond which they were scattered. Masada stands for an ineffaceable value in the history and culture of a peoples, a daily reaffirmation of freedom and dignity. « Masada shall not fall again », the ritual phrase pronounced every year by the young Israeli recruits during an impressive military ceremony held there, rings out as a warning and a promise.

Our knowledge of Masada and the dramatic events which took place within its walls is thanks to the historian Flavius Josephus, in Hebrew Yosef ben Matatyahu, born in 37 A.D. into an important family of priests, and for a time head of the resistance of his people against Rome.

Taken prisoner in 67 A.D. in the city of Iotapata, he was converted to the politics of Vespasian and became one of his most convinced champions. He moved to Rome where he wrote his principal works, « *The Jewish Wars* » between 75 and 79, and « *The Jewish Antiquities* » between 93 and 94, which reveal a direct and anguished participation as well as being well documented faithful chronicles.

The fortress of Masada looms over an overwhelmingly desolate landscape hemmed in on the top of a massive rocky outcrop overhanging the Dead Sea, four hundred meters above the western banks.

Still today, as in the days when Flavius Josephus wrote, there are two places where it can be climbed. « *Of these two points, one is to the east, at the end of a path which rises from the Asphaltite lake, the other is to the west... The first of these two paths is called « the snake path » on account of its narrowness and continuous turns... After a distance of thirty stadia the path reaches the summit, which does not terminate in a peak but in a flat open space. The first to build a fortress here was the high priest Jonathan, and he called*

The haunting landscape with the Dead Sea seen from the top of the citadel.

The exterior of the building housing the Mikve.

it Masada. » At present we tend to believe that Jonathan can be identified with Alexander Jannaois. The name Masada seems to derive from « metzuda » which means « mountain castle ». After this, in the history of Masada, the great king and tireless builder Herod enters the scene. In his efforts to safeguard himself from the twofold danger of the Judeans who might rise up and restore the preceding dynasty and of Cleopatra who unfailingly incited Antony to eliminate Herod so she could have the kingdom of Judea, he decided to fortify Masada, and built there not one but two palaces and a series of buildings which would have made the citadel practically impregnable.

« In fact all around the top he raised a wall built of white stone seven stadia long, twelve cubits high and eight in thickness, from which rose 37 towers each 50 cubits high... ». This was a casemate wall, that is a double wall in which the intervening space was divided into various units which served a military use. When the Zealots barricaded themselves in Masada for their last stand, they occupied these premises, where afterwards many objects of daily use came to light: containers for unguents, make-up boxes, pieces of cloth, etc. The likelihood of having to remain in Masada at

length had led Herod to take all possible precautions, such as that of storing up all kinds of staples. « The excellent quality and good preservation of the supplies which had been stored there was even more surprising: in fact a great quantity of wheat, enough for a long time, was found stored there, an abundance of wine and oil and moreover all kinds of legumes and piles of dates... ». The storerooms were easy to identify because of their long narrow shape, without openings. Numerous containers were found, varying in form according to their original contents: wine, oil, flour, etc.

THE ROYAL PALACES

An authentic royal citadel, Masada actually had two palaces, even if Flavius Josephus cited only one: « He then also built a palace at the edge of the slopes on the west, at a lower level than the enclosing walls and facing south... Inside, the construction of the rooms, of the porticoes, of the baths was varied and extremely rich: everywhere there were columns made of a single piece of stone while the walls and pavements of the rooms were covered with variegated stones... ».

Traces of the Roman encampment dating to the siege of the fortress are clearly visible in the superb landscape which surrounds Masada.

The fortress of Masada.

The imposing access Ramp built by the Romans seen from the side and from above: this was the only way to overcome the resistence of Masada.

The two palaces had been built with all possible comfort and luxury: one stood to the west and was the official palace of Herod, where the ceremonies took place; the other, the so-called Hanging Palace, was to the north, and was built in three levels excavated in the rock and was the most spectacular. The upper terrace was to all extents an extension of the top of the mountain, a « prow » of rock launched into the void: it is the highest point of Masada, from where the eye embraces a panorama of rare beauty and fascina-

tion. The actual residential sector of the royal family, probably built for Herod alone or for him and one of his nine wives, was here. The apartments were situated under a large semicircular portico: unfortunately the decoration once to be found on the walls and ceilings of these rooms has all been lost. Twenty meters further down was the intermediate terrace, the premises of which — like the preceding — were destined for the entertainment and relaxation of the sovereign. The remains of the circular construction provide us with an idea of what the building must originally have looked like: the two concentric walls served as base for the two rows of columns which supported the roof, probably of wood. Invisible from the outside, a staircase joined this level

The cableway that joins Masada to the plain.

Two views of the « Bianca », the ramp built by the Romans in their siege of the citadel.

The Byzantine gate built over the ruins of an earlier gate dating to Herod's time.

to the other two.

About 33 meters further down was the lower terrace: here we are at about 330 meters above the Dead Sea and the eye can freely roam from Ein Gedi up to the heights of Mount Moab, on the opposite shore of the sea.

The baths which Herod had had built here are a typical example of a style which at the time was highly fashionable throughout the provinces of the Roman empire. The lower part of the wall was covered by a layer of plaster which the artists then manipulated so that it looked like marble with its characteristic veining. It is also thanks to the extremely dry climate of Masada that these paintings have survived in good state up to

Exterior of a tower of Herod's palace: the mosaic pavement inside reflects the folk art motifs of the Jews of the time.

now. Herod's baths were conceived in the best tradition of the Roman baths: in fact they had a frigidarium, a tepidarium and a calidarium.

All this makes one reflect on the problems Herod's engineers faced regarding the water supply, for there were no springs near Masada, and it rarely rained. The solution was genial, even if implementing it was anything but easy. It meant exploiting the two wadi or gulleys which ran to the north and south of the rock of Masada, and building two dams to « harness » the flood waters. From here, a system of open channels took the water to a series of twelve cisterns dug into the rock, which in turn supplied the various rooms.

The palace seen from the west and a lovely mosaic with geometric motifs.

The apse of the Byzantine church.

Another entrance gate to Masada dating to Byzantine times.

Every cistern had a capacity of 4000 cubic meters: truly remarkable, so much so that Flavius Josephus went so far as to say that the water supply was « *in quantity no less than that of those who had springs at their disposal* ».

This allowed Herod to build a second bath complex, adjacent to the north palace, and whose existence was revealed to the archaeologists by the discovery of about two hundred small clay columns, typical of a hypocaust, where water was poured on the hot pavement to create a steam bath. This complex also had a frigidarium, tepidarium, calidarium and an apodyterium, where clothing was deposited.

Herod's other palace was, as we have said, the one destined for official ceremonies. Situated to the west, it is the largest building in Masada, with an area of circa 3500 square meters. One wing was destined for the service rooms, another for the residential quarters,

כנסיה
ביזאנטית
BYZANTINE
CHURCH

4

השער הביזאנטי
אל מצדה
נבנה על חורבות שער
הרודיאני
THE BYZANTINE GATE
TO MASADA BUILT
OVER RUINS OF A
HERODIAN GATE

5

A general view and a detail of the « columbarium », perhaps used to contain the ashes of the non-Hebrew soldiers who died at Masada.

The synagogue of Masada is the oldest discovered in Israel and was built in the period of the Second Temple.

and still another for administrative purposes and storerooms.

The palace also had a bathing pool, situated at the bottom of a plastered staircase which made it possible to bathe even in a limited amount of water. Before entering the pool the bathers left their clothing in the niches dug into the walls. One of the loveliest colored mosaics in all of Israel was discovered in this palace: made of blue, black, red and white tesserae, it was inspired by the typical plant motifs of Hebrew art, the pomegranate, the olive branch and grape leaves, together with geometric decorations which consisted of a play of intersecting circles and squares.

In the period between Herod and the Roman siege, the rock of Masada was never uninhabited. The buildings erected by Herod were reused, and to all effects no other buildings were added, aside from those built for specific purposes, such as the Synagogue and the

« Mikve », added by the Zealots when they arrived in Masada. The latter, that is the ritual bath, presented the same problems Herod's engineers had had to face. Zealot rites required immersion in pure water (« Mikve »), that is rain water that had not been in contact with various transportation vessels. On the other hand, however, the Hebrew law itself allowed that it was sufficient to have one part of « pure » water to which other water could be added, purifying it by contact. Three pools had thus been built, two large ones and a small one: rain water was collected in the largest basin, while the water from the cisterns was brought to the other two. The bather washed in the small « impure » pool before entering the large « pure » one: at that point, via a connecting channel the rain water flowed in and purified the other water so that the ritual immersion could finally take place.

On these pages, three pictures of the tower overlooking the storerooms.

Crowd of tourists on the ruins of Masada.

A rocky cleft under the excavations of Masada.

A corner of the excavations of the citadel, near the
« water gate »

THE SYNAGOGUE

The other building dating to the time of the Zealots was the synagogue: and that it was a synagogue is revealed by the presence of benches around a central clearing and above all by the eastern orientation of the building towards Jerusalem. Since it dates to the period of the Second Temple, it is the oldest synagogue discovered in Israel. It served as such also during Herod's period, for it is known that the king arrived here with many persons of Hebrew faith among the members of his court.

However, before the Zealots arrived, the building had been used as stables by the Roman garrison, as can be deduced from the traces of animal excrements found on the pavement. During the excavations, numerous fragments of jars, which had held Italian wine for the king, also came to light. An inscription reads « to king Herod of Judea ». Another shard bears the date of the year 19 A.D. and the name of the consul C. Sentius Saturninus.

THE SIEGE OF MASADA

And thus we reach the last chapter in the history of Masada, the most famous, the most dramatic.

Once more it is Flavius Josephus who tells us what happened. « *In the meanwhile, after Bassus died, the command of Judea feel to Flavius Silvus. The latter, seeing that all the rest of the land had been subdued with arms with the exception of a single fortress that was still in the hands of the rebels, called together all the forces that were in the region and moved against it* ». Flavius Silvus was an astute and intelligent soldier, and when, in the spring of 70 A.D. he moved with his X Legion — the Fretensis, with all of 10,000 men — against Masada, he was well aware that the pocket of resistence barricaded at the summit of the mountain would not easily fall. Not only were the 960 people up there — men, women, children and old people — excellent fighters, but they also had'enough food and water to enable them to withstand a long siege. This was why he decided to take Masada by storm.

41

On these pages, four pictures of the building housing
the Baths: the external tower, the entrance, the
« calidarium » and the remains of a fresco.

His first task was that of rendering any attempt at
flight by those besieged impossible and he therefore
built a long wall all around the rock, a meter and
eighty thick, reinforced by twelve towers about one
hundred meters apart, and by eight entrenched fields,
two larger ones and six smaller ones. The larger ones
measured 140 by 180 meters and the smaller ones 130
by 160. Their state of preservation is practically per-
fect, as can be realized by looking down from the top
of the citadel. « *After having surrounded the entire
place with a line of circumvallation... the Roman com-
mander began the siege operations in the only place
which he had found suitable for the elevation of a rampart... a large rocky prominence of notable width and
height rose up... it was called "Bianca" (White)* ».
Still today those who arrive at Masada are struck by
the blinding whiteness of the siege ramp: without
doubt we are in the presence of one of the best

An allover view of the storerooms.

Almost camouflaged in the rock of Masada, the sinuous
« snake path » leading to the top can just be made out.

Reconstruction of the Hanging Palace.

preserved military works of antiquity, and cannot help
but admire the construction endeavors which this
ramp required.

Flavius Josephus says that the summit of the ramp did
not reach all the way to the casemate wall, but stopped
about « *300 cubits further down* », about one hundred
and fifty meters. Then « *Silvas... ordered the army to
build on it a rampart... and on top was built a plat-
form of large blocks joined together... and moreover
a tower of 60 cubits all covered with iron was built,
from the top of which the Romans, shooting with a
large number of catapults, soon made a clean sweep of
the defenders of the wall and stopped anyone from
showing themselves. At the same time Silvus, who had
also built a large battering ram, gave orders to con-
tinuously attack the wall and at the end, although after
great endeavors, he succeeded in opening a breach and
getting it to fall* ». Hundreds of these shot, at least as

The circular structure of the
intermediate terrace: the two
concentric walls served as base for
two rows of columns which
supported the roof.

Bird's-eye view and two shots of the
lower terrace.

The lower terrace of Herod's palace: the wall paintings have been preserved thanks to the dry climate of Masada.

large as grapefruits, have been found near the west gate, at the very place where the Romans concentrated their attack. Silva then ordered torches to be launched against the wooden partitions which the Zealots had hastily elevated to ward off the Roman attack and at the beginning it seemed that fate was coming to the aid of the besieged, for a wind rose from the north which blew the flames towards the Romans, causing some panic. « ...then suddenly, as if it were the will of the gods, a gust of wind came up from the south and, blowing violently from the opposite direction, pushed the fire against the wall, which by then went up in flames from one end to the other ».

At this point it became clear to the Zealots that Masada was lost and while outside the fortress this imposing military action was taking place, within the walls one of the most moving tragedies in the history of man was unfolding. Fearful of Roman retaliation and dreading above all that the members of their families would be

בית מפואר
VILLA

20

מחצבה
QUARRY

21

A corner of a building and the entrance to a quarry.

The exterior wall of building VIII.

enslaved, the combatants of Masada chose collective suicide to being captured alive by the enemy.

Eleazar ben Yair, the head of the Zealots, used highly dramatic tones to convince his followers of the extreme sacrifice: « *May our wives die without being dishonored and our children without submitting to slavery and after their end let us exchange a generous service preserving our liberty as our sepulchral garments. But first let us destroy by fire both our possessions and the fortress... let us set apart only our stocks of food, which after our death will testify that we did not fall for lack of food but because we preferred death to slavery, faithful to the choice we made at the beginning... Let us make haste to leave them (the Romans) in amazement at our death and in admiration for our courage* ».

And it was amazement and admiration that the Romans felt when the next day, in a deathly silence, they entered the fortress. Inside Masada lay the lifeless bodies of the 960 Zealots, men, women, children and old people, reunited in their last embrace.

With touching realism, through the account of one of the survivors, Flavius Josephus tells us what had happened: « *While they caressed and embraced their wives and held children aloft in their arms weeping and kissing them for the last time, at the same time... all killed their dear ones, one after the other... Then, unable to bear the anguish of what they had done and feeling they would offend the dead if they continued to live, they hastened to pile their belongings in a single pile and set fire to it; then having chosen lots as to which of them would kill all the others, they lay down next to the bodies of their wives and children and embraced them as they bared their throats to those charged with killing them. ...The survivors decided to draw lots and the one chosen by fate was to kill the other nine and finally himself. At the end the nine bared their throats to their companion who, when he was sole survivor,*

Bird's-eye view of building IX, where the families of the officers leaved.

Exterior of building XII, residence of the royal family.

A corner of Herod's palace.

first looked round at all the dead... and, when he was certain they were all dead, set fire to the palace, and gathering together whatever strength remained, plunged his sword into his body up to its hilt and fell down heavily next to his relatives. Nine hundred and sixty were the victims... and the date of the massacre was the 15 of the month of Xanthico ». It was the day after Easter of the year 73 A.D.: the siege had lasted three years.

Two women and five children had managed to save themselves from this massacre by hiding in underground passageways and they were thus able to tell the speechless Romans about the last hours of the resistance of Masada. This was also confirmed by the moving discovery of eleven small shards: each one bore a different name, among which that of « Ben Yair ». Archaeologists rightly believed that they had found the shards the last courageous heroes of Masada had used to cast lots.

THE DISCOVERY OF MASADA

Thanks to the writings of Flavius Josephus it had long been known that the citadel of Masada existed but the exact site had never been located. In 1807 a traveler named Seetzen had seen the ruins on the rock while he was in a boat out in the Dead Sea but he had mistakenly identified them with the city of Zif.
It was not until 1938 that the site was correctly identified as Masada.
Two American travellers, Edward Robinson and E. Smith, who happened to be in Ein Gedi observed that rocky outcrop which the Arabs called Sebbeh from a distance and wrote in their travel journal: « We were greatly struck by its aspect and examining it with a telescope succeeded in distinguishing what seemed to be a building on the north-western part and traces of other constructions further to the east... further investigation makes it possible to affirm without a doubt

The « columbarium » and the stairs that lead to one of the cisterns of Masada.

that it is the site of the ancient and famous fortress of Masada… ».

The first to climb the rocky outcrop and visit the ruins were the American missionary S.W. Wollcott and the English painter Tipping, in 1842. The two travellers confirmed the precision of Flavius Josephus' tale, identifying among others, Silvus' general headquarters, in the camp F. In the years that followed, more and more travellers adventured to Masada: in January 1851, the Frenchman F. de Saulcy, who climbed up via the siege ramp; in 1867, the Englishman Warren, who however climbed it from the eastern side and discovered the « snake path »; in 1905 the system of water supply was discovered by Sandel, and in 1932 it was the turn of the complex of the Roman camps, thanks to Szoltan, who was helped in this by the publication of a series of aerial photographs taken in the years 1924-28 by English pilots of the RAF.

Two pictures of the pool, with the stairs that led into the water.

The first real archaeological campaign, precise and scientific, took place between 1963 and 1965, under the direction of the Hebrew University of Jerusalem, the Israel Exploration Society and the Department of Antiquity of the Ministry of Education and Culture. Hundreds and hundreds of volunteers came from all parts of the world to work here, often having to endure discomforts and privations, under the direction of the great archaeologist Yigal Yadin. In real life their jobs and professions ranged from one extreme to the other, they spoke the most varied languages and dialects, but each of them shared something that was more than simply love for archaeology and the appeal of rediscovery. It was Masada that had called them from every part of the earth, it was Masada that now united them with its archaeological, historical and symbolical importance, it was Masada which had taken a place in their hearts and conscience.

The entrance to the kibbutz of Ein Gedi and a corner of the pool.

EIN GEDI

A purely descriptive reference to this site is to be found in a passage of that splendid allegory known as the Song of Solomon: « *My beloved is unto me as a cluster of camphire in the vineyards of Ein-Gedi* ». (Solomon, 1:14). And still another quote, this time rigorously historical, in the *I Book of Samuel* (24:1 ff), where David flees from Saul. « *And David went up from thence, and dwelt in strong holds at Ein-Gedi.* » (23:29) « *And it came to pass, when Saul was returned from following the Philistines, that it was told him, saying, Behold, David is in the wilderness of Ein-Gedi. Then Saul took three thousand chosen men out of all Israel, and went to seek David and his men upon the rocks of the wild goats. And he came to the sheepcotes by the way* » (24:1-3).

Ein Gedi is about eighty kilometers from Jerusalem, on the road that skirts the Dead Sea on its way to Eilat, on the Red Sea. In Hebrew the name means « goat's spring », but also « spring of the young boy »: both definitions are valid for this marvelous place, whether because of the antelope and gazelles that have been here since Biblical times, or because of the episode of the young David. It has also been identified with the locality of Haze-zon-tamar, when it is mentioned in Genesis (14:7) « ... *they... smote all the country of the Amalekites, and also the Amorites, that dwelt in Haze-zon-tamar* ».

From earliest times the extraordinary climatic conditions and the exceptional fertility of the soil had favored the settlement of agrarian communities here: archaeological excavations have brought to light the remains of a Chalcolithic temple, at least 6000 years old. Ever since antiquity the abundance of springs has made it possible to cultivate a variety of products such

Antilopes and gazelles in the wildlife reserve of Ein Gedi.

Two pictures of the thriving vegetation of the oasis of Ein Gedi.

as dates, bananas, grapes, cotton, roses, so much so that during the siege of Masada the Romans came here to stock up on their provisions.

In the Natural Park of Ein Gedi, which covers about 450 hectares, are four springs: Ein Gedi, which gives its name to the park, Nahal Arugot to the south, Ein Shulamit and that of Nahal David, which forms a beautiful waterfall 185 meters high that falls into a natural pool where one can bathe. The vegetation is typically sub-tropical: azaleas, bamboos, the henna plant. Antelopes, gazelles and ibex fearlessly cross the road or peer out — quite unafraid — from between the rocks which flank the paths that cross the park.

Near the park, in the midst of the desert, is the kibbutz of Ein Gedi, created in 1953. Today the kibbutz has a restaurant, guest houses, a swimming pool and a well-equipped bathing establishment.

The mountains of Jordan can be glimpsed beyond the
Dead Sea.

DEAD SEA

A legend narrates that during the siege of Jerusalem,
in 70 A.D., various slaves were condemned to death
and were put in shackles and thrown from the heights
of Mount Moab into the sea below. But the prisoners
did not drown and every time they were thrown into
the water, they returned to the surface. The fact so im-
pressed the Romans, that the slaves were pardoned.
The Biblical « sea of salt » lies at the bottom of a tec-
tonic trench that was formed between the end of the
Tertiary period and the beginning of the Quaternary
(more than two million years ago), about 400 meters
below the level of the Mediterranean. In that period a
terrifying cataclysm took place which resulted in the
so-called Great Rift Valley, which begins in Asia
Minor, at the foot of the Taurus mountain chain, and
crosses the Red Sea all the way to Kenya.
The entire valley of the Jordan is nothing but a tiny
part of this immense fissure in the earth's crust.
This enormous lake — for it is none other than a lake,
since on the north the Jordan empties into it, but there
is no outlet on the south — has a greater solid content
than any other body of water: 25%, above all of potas-
sium chloride, an enormous amount in comparison to
the 4% to 6% that ocean water normally contains. The
high rate of evaporation, about eight million cubic
meters of water a day, is the result of the implacable
sun as it burns down from a motionless dazzling sky,
summer and winter. The water is therefore surprisingly
dense, ten times greater than ordinary water. This ex-
plains its characteristic bitter taste and oily texture.
One can bathe in the waters of the Dead Sea but only
by taking the necessary precautions, for despite the fact
that it is easy to float in this dense liquid, the high salt
content can irritate the more sensitive parts of the face.

In antiquity mention was already made of poisonous gases emitted by the sea and of the birds who were unable to reach the opposite shore because they fell dead into the water.

There is nothing, absolutely nothing alive in this sea: neither fish, nor algae, nor mollusks, only rocks and salt, candid saline formations which rise from the water like ghostly coral. The air too is different, oppressive and heavy, with an odor of sulphur and petroleum. Josephus Flavius called it « Lacus Asphaltites »; the Bible speaks of these waters with floating patches of bitumen which the Egyptians imported in the 4th century B.C. to embalm their dead.

On the other hand, these same physical-chemical characteristics furnish the waters of the Dead Sea with

A must for every tourist: the Dead Sea lies at the lowest point of the earth's surface, 398 meters below the level of the sea.

Three pictures of the Dead Sea and its candid saline formations.

therapeutic virtues and they are particularly suitable for curing various skin diseases. Moreover, the dry climate and the oxygen-rich atmosphere are indicated in curing diseases of the respiratory tract. Mineral salts are at present extracted by the Jordan plants, which are on the east banks, and by the Israeli plants on the southern bank.

This region numbers various interesting records: despite a minimum fluctuation in the level of the sea, with its depth in the north zone of 430 meters it remains the lowest point on the Earth; the atmospheric pressure there is the highest on our planet and there is 15% more oxygen in its atmosphere than there is in the Mediterranean.

The Dead Sea is particularly famous for the ease with which one can float in its waters and for the mud which is used in beauty treatments.

A view of the beach of Ein Gedi.

The rocky formation near Sodom known as « Lot's wife ».

It is here, at the southern extremity of the Dead Sea, that tradition sets the story of Sodom and Gomorrah, annihilated by the flood of fire and brimstone sent down by an irate God.

« *And Abraham... looked toward Sodom and Gomorrah, and toward all the land of the plain, and beheld, and, lo, the smoke of the country went up as the smoke of a furnace* ». (Genesis, 19:28). With this famous passage of the Bible in mind, it occurred to a scientist that in all likelihood this fire referred to the presence of telluric gases, and that where these are to be found there was also petroleum. This hypothesis became a certainty when, on November 3, 1953, the first Israeli oil well was sunk in this area.

CONTENTS